Today's Superst☆rs
Entertainment

Jamie Foxx

by Geoffrey M. Horn

GARETHSTEVENS
GS
PUBLISHING
A Member of the WRC Media Family of Companies

Please visit our web site at: www.garethstevens.com
For a free color catalog describing our list of high-quality books,
call 1-800-542-2595 (USA) or 1-800-387-3178 (Canada).

Library of Congress Cataloging-in-Publication Data

Horn, Geoffrey M.
    Jamie Foxx / by Geoffrey M. Horn.
        p. cm. — (Today's superstars. Entertainment)
    Includes bibliographical references and index.
    ISBN-13: 978-0-8368-4232-6 (lib. bdg.)
    ISBN-10: 0-8368-4232-4 (lib. bdg.)
    1. Foxx, Jamie—Juvenile literature. 2. Actors—United States—
Biography—Juvenile literature. I. Title.
PN2287.F632H67   2005
792.02'8'092—dc22
    [B]   2005049041

This edition first published in 2006 by
Gareth Stevens Publishing
A Weekly Reader® Company
1 Reader's Digest Road
Pleasantville, NY 10570-7000 USA

This edition copyright © 2006 by Gareth Stevens, Inc.

Editor: Jim Mezzanotte
Art direction and design: Tammy West
Picture research: Diane Laska-Swanke

Photo credits: Cover, pp. 5, 7 © Kevin Winter/Getty Images; pp. 10, 12
© Mike Fuentes/Getty Images; p. 14 © Pete Mitchell/WireImage.com;
pp. 17, 20, 23, 25, 26 Photofest; p. 22 © Mike Guastella/WireImage.com;
p. 28 © Frank Micelotta/Getty Images

Printed in the United States of America

2 3 4 5 6 7 8 9 10 09 08 07

Contents

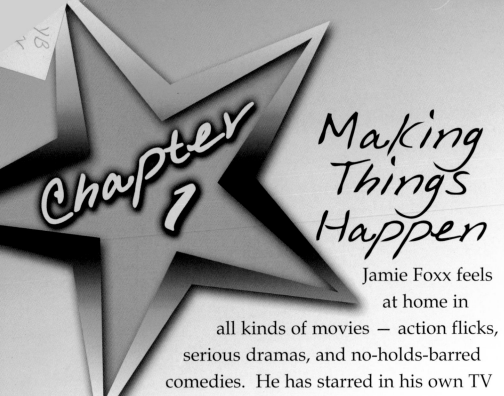

Chapter 1

Making Things Happen

Jamie Foxx feels at home in all kinds of movies — action flicks, serious dramas, and no-holds-barred comedies. He has starred in his own TV sitcom. On the same series, he was also a writer, director, and producer. Jamie has done stand-up comedy shows on cable TV. He's recorded his own hit tunes. Is there anything the man can't do?

"As a comedian, as an actor, you've got to make things happen," he says. "You've got to have a lot of things in the air."

Few actors achieve in a lifetime what Jamie did in a single year. In 2004, he starred in four movies, and three of them competed for major honors. He won an NAACP Image

Fact File

Jamie was nominated for Golden Globe Awards for *Redemption*, *Collateral*, and *Ray*. He was also nominated for three awards by the Screen Actors Guild (SAG). *Ray* was the charm. The film earned him the Golden Globe and SAG trophies, as well as an Oscar.

Saying No to Gangs

Redemption is based on a true story. In the movie, Jamie Foxx plays Stanley "Tookie" Williams. In 1971, Tookie and others founded the Crips gang. Ten years later, he was sentenced to die for killing four people. During his years on death row, Tookie had a change of heart. He realized that gang-banging was wrong. He wrote books to convince kids not to join gangs. For his work to stop gang violence, he has been nominated for the Nobel Peace Prize.

On Tookie's web site, he apologizes for all the harm he caused. He writes that he "didn't expect the Crips to end up ruining the lives of so many young people, especially young black men who have hurt other young black men.... I no longer participate in the so-called gangster lifestyle, and I deeply regret that I ever did.... I pray that one day my apology will be accepted. I also pray that your suffering, caused by gang violence, will soon come to an end as more gang members wake up and stop hurting themselves and others."

Jamie shows off his Golden Globe Award for *Ray*.

Award for his performance in *Redemption*, a made-for-TV movie. For his supporting role in the movie *Collateral*, a thriller, he was nominated for an Oscar. (He lost to Morgan Freeman in *Million Dollar Baby*.)

Jamie's biggest score was for *Ray*, a film about the life of singer Ray Charles. Even before the movie came out, some people said Jamie might win an Oscar for it — and he did. For his wonderful work in *Ray*, Jamie won an Oscar for Best Actor. His acting in that film also earned him a shelf full of other prizes.

One Man, Many Talents

Acting in serious films was only part of what Jamie did in 2004. He also starred in a romantic comedy, *Breakin' All the Rules*. It wasn't a big hit at the box office. But Jamie got good reviews, even from movie critics who didn't say many kind things about the movie.

Jamie's career as a singer and songwriter got a big boost in 2004. He signed a deal with J Records

Fact File

At the Nickelodeon Kids' Choice show in 2005, Jamie won the Hidden Talent Award. His hidden talent? Rolling his eyes in opposite directions!

Album Buzz

Jamie has a lot of material for his first album on J Records. He jokes that he's "got, like, 30,000 tracks." He's been working with 50 Cent, Kanye West, Snoop Dogg, and other top artists of today. But Jamie's own musical tastes are old school. "We're gonna get back to love music," he says. "Young love music that old people can appreciate."

A "hidden talent" earned Jamie a 2005 Kids' Choice Award on Nickelodeon.

and began working on an album of his own songs. Later that year, he was nominated for a Grammy Award for "Slow Jamz." He performed on the song with Twista and Kanye West. The cut appeared on Twista's *Kamikaze* album and Kanye West's *The College Dropout*.

In February 2005, Jamie was featured on the Grammy Awards ceremony. At one point, he joined R&B star Alicia Keys on stage, and the two performed a touching tribute to Ray Charles. Alicia took home four Grammy Awards that night. She had warm praise for Jamie's talents. "When we got together you could just feel his passion for music," she told a reporter. "I mean, he's good — he plays for real. He doesn't just kind-of sort-of play. He plays for real and he sings for real."

Alicia could have been talking about Jamie's whole career as an artist. Jamie has many talents. But these days, no matter what he does, he always plays for real.

Fact File

Jamie's first music CD, *Peep This*, came out in 1994. The album sold about 300,000 copies.

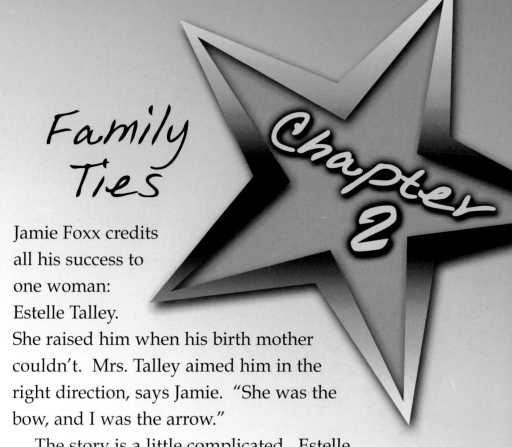

Family Ties

Chapter 2

Jamie Foxx credits all his success to one woman: Estelle Talley. She raised him when his birth mother couldn't. Mrs. Talley aimed him in the right direction, says Jamie. "She was the bow, and I was the arrow."

The story is a little complicated. Estelle Talley and her husband Mark lived in Terrell, Texas. Years before Jamie was born, they adopted a young girl named Louise. Louise was still a teenager when she became pregnant. On December 13, 1967, she gave birth to a baby boy.

The boy was called Eric Morlon Bishop. The last name came from his father, Darrell Bishop. Louise and Darrell broke up when the baby was only seven months old. They gave the baby to the Talleys, who adopted him as their son.

Mother and Son

The Talleys adopted both Louise and her son, so Jamie's family tree looks very unusual. Jamie points out that Mrs. Talley was both his grandmother and his mother. He also notes that his birth mother is also his sister. Jamie had contact with both his birth parents while he was growing up. He saw Louise more often than he saw Darrell. But Jamie and Louise still aren't as close as he'd like. "One day we'll really, really, really be mother and son," he said in 2001. "It's not quite like that right now. But I think all things happen in time."

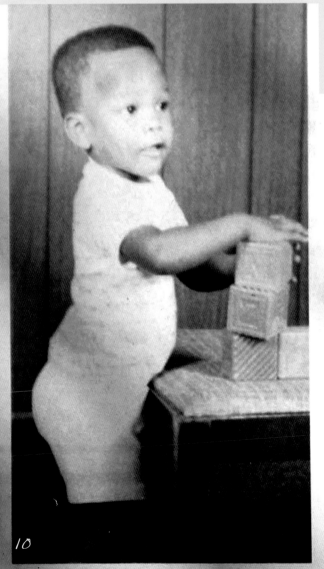

In high school, Jamie was still known as Eric Bishop. Mrs. Talley put this message in his 1986 yearbook.

Eric, I have watched you grow during the last 17 years. I am very proud of your accomplishments. Life is a road of trials and errors, and the path is just beginning. When the path grows dark just remember to ask God for help.
Love, Granny

The Talleys still called the boy Eric Bishop. He was known by that name as long as he lived in Terrell. It was only later, after he moved to California, that he changed his name to Jamie Foxx.

Estelle Talley loved the church. She went to church almost every Sunday. She made sure young Eric went, too. She also made him practice the piano. When Eric was five years old, he started taking piano lessons from a Dallas music teacher.

Mark Talley didn't talk much. Jamie recalls him saying maybe a few hundred words his whole life. "The one thing he could do was whup yo' ass," Jamie says. "And when I say he whupped it, he wh-whupped it."

The Talleys may have been strict. But Jamie is grateful to them for giving him a loving and stable home. "I have never had a bad day, really, in my life," he says.

Hometown Hero
To be popular in school, it helps if you're good

Fact File

Eric and his friends started an R&B band called Leather and Lace. He wore his hair curled like his musical idol, Lionel Richie. Richie reached his peak in 1983 with the album *Can't Slow Down* and the number-one pop singles "All Night Long" and "Hello."

Talking with Mrs. Talley

Jamie was only seventeen when Mark Talley died. But Estelle Talley didn't pass away until October 2004, at the age of ninety-five. When Jamie accepted an Oscar four months later, he called Mrs. Talley his "first acting teacher."

"She told me to stand up straight," he said. "Put your shoulders back. Act like you got some sense.... She said I want you to be a southern gentleman. She still talks to me now. Only now, she talks to me in my dreams. And I can't wait to go to sleep tonight because we got a lot to talk about."

In this yearbook photo, Jamie's hair is curled like that of his musical idol, Lionel Richie.

at music, sports, or being funny. As a teenager, Eric Bishop was successful at all three. Being good-looking didn't hurt, either.

By the time Eric was fifteen years old, he was earning three hundred dollars a month to play piano at several different churches. Mrs. Talley insisted that he give her all the money he earned. At the time, he thought she was the meanest woman in the world. Only later did he find out that she had put every penny in a savings account under his name.

Eric played quarterback for the Terrell Tigers, his high school football team. He set a school record in his senior year by passing for more than a thousand yards. He also competed in basketball, baseball, and track. On the school bus or in the classroom, he was always cracking jokes. He had a real gift for mimicry. But his small Texas town didn't have much to offer a budding young comic. Besides, Mrs. Talley wanted him to get a college degree.

After graduating from high school, Eric majored

Fact File

Jamie recorded a special video message for his hometown fans on Oscar night in 2005. "I've never turned my back on Terrell, Texas," he said. "And Terrell, Texas, has never turned its back on me."

in classical piano at a college in San Diego, California. It didn't take him long to realize the place wasn't right for him. Classical music was tough — too tough. He could always head home to Terrell. But if he wanted to stay in California, he would need to find a different path to success.

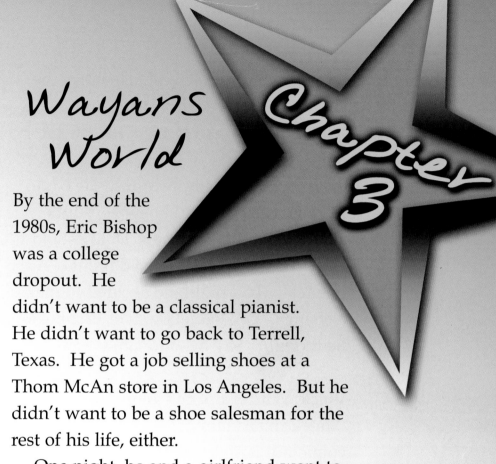

Wayans World

Chapter 3

By the end of the
1980s, Eric Bishop
was a college
dropout. He
didn't want to be a classical pianist.
He didn't want to go back to Terrell,
Texas. He got a job selling shoes at a
Thom McAn store in Los Angeles. But he
didn't want to be a shoe salesman for the
rest of his life, either.

One night, he and a girlfriend went to
an L.A. comedy club. He had always been
able to make his friends laugh. How about
a room full of strangers? It was open-mike
night, and his girlfriend challenged him to
go up on stage. He took the dare.

He started off with an impression of
Bill Cosby. The crowd loved it. Next, he
did Ronald Reagan. A young black dude
imitating an elderly former president?
The audience roared with laughter.

"It was the most incredible feeling," he later told *Texas Monthly* magazine. "It was, okay, I think I know what I want to be right now."

Eric could do impressions. He could tell jokes. But he still knew very little about the craft of comedy. Doing stand-up, he had good nights and bad nights. After one really bad night, he decided to make a change. I've had enough of Eric Bishop, he thought. Say hello to Jamie Foxx.

Black, White, and in Color
Appearing as Jamie Foxx, the young comic put it all together. Soon, he was earning thousands of dollars a week.

In 1991, Jamie joined the cast of *In Living Color*. It was the hippest and blackest show on network TV. Keenen Ivory Wayans created the series, and other members of the Wayans family starred in it. Another regular on the show was a talented white comic, little known at the time. His name was Jim Carrey.

Fact File

Bill Cosby was one of the most popular comics of the 1980s. His top-rated sitcom, *The Cosby Show*, ran from 1984 to 1992.

From Clark Kent to Superman

"Eric Bishop is Clark Kent," Jamie says, "and Jamie Foxx is Superman." But why did the superstar choose that particular name? The answer may surprise you. When Jamie was first doing stand-up, more men than women wanted to do it. If a man signed up at a comedy club, he couldn't be sure he'd get called. But when a woman put her name down, she almost always got to perform.

One night, Eric Bishop signed up at a comedy club using three separate names: Tracy, Stacy, and Jamie. These names were unisex — they could be used by a woman or a man. True to form, the name Jamie was called early. But it wasn't a woman who took the stage. Jamie was sharp that night, and the name stuck. He took the last name Foxx as a tribute to a popular black comic, Redd Foxx. Redd's original name was John Elroy Sanford. He starred in the 1970s TV sitcom *Sanford and Son*. Redd died in 1991.

Wearing a dress and a blond wig, Jamie (as Wanda) wanted to "rock your world" on the TV show *In Living Color*.

For Jamie, *In Living Color* was like a college of comedy. He says seven or eight people on that show were funnier than he was. Jamie learned something about comedy from each of them. For example, he told *People* magazine that Damon Wayans taught him "the importance of having a little attitude."

Jamie's best-known character on the show was Ugly Wanda. To play Wanda, he put on a dress, wore a blond wig, and loaded up on padding and lipstick. Everything about Wanda was big — her lips, her hips, her chest, her needs. "I'm gonna rock your world," she told any man she wanted to get next to.

Jamie thinks he knows what made Wanda so popular. He told *Texas Monthly*, "I think what it was, was she would actually get sad. She had emotions. She was a woman."

Fact File

The Wayans family had a big comedy hit in 2000 with *Scary Movie*. Keenen Ivory Wayans directed the film, and Shawn Wayans and Marlon Wayans starred in it. The movie, which cost less than $20 million to make, earned more than $150 million in the United States alone.

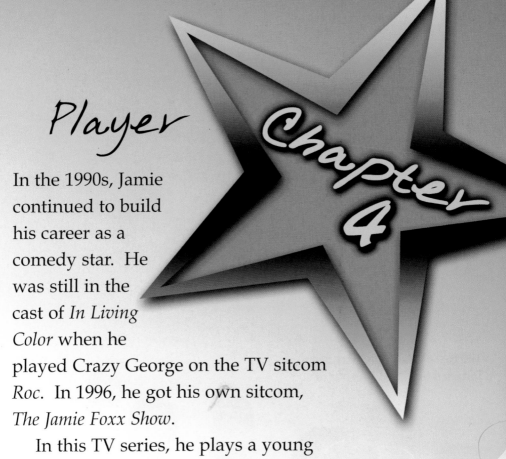

Player

In the 1990s, Jamie continued to build his career as a comedy star. He was still in the cast of *In Living Color* when he played Crazy George on the TV sitcom *Roc*. In 1996, he got his own sitcom, *The Jamie Foxx Show*.

In this TV series, he plays a young Texan who comes to California seeking fame and fortune in show business. While waiting for his big break, he takes a job at an L.A. hotel run by his aunt and uncle. Jamie freely admits the shows weren't always top-notch. But the series was popular enough to run for five seasons. In 1998, Jamie won an NAACP Image Award for his work on the program.

On the big screen, Jamie played Bunz in

Fact File

A regular on *The Jamie Foxx Show* was the comic actor Garrett Morris. Morris has had a long career in TV and movies. He was a cast member of *Saturday Night Live* when that show first aired in 1975.

Knight Moves

One of the best episodes of *The Jamie Foxx Show* was "Save the Drama for Your Mama." It aired at the end of the first season. This episode featured singer Gladys Knight as Jamie's mother. The highlight came when the two of them sang a duet. She sang another duet with Jamie on her 2001 album, *At Last.*

Back in the 1960s, Gladys Knight and the Pips were a top Motown group. They had their biggest hit in 1967 with "I Heard It Through the Grapevine," later a hit for Marvin Gaye. Gladys Knight and the Pips entered the Rock and Roll Hall of Fame in 1996. Gladys released a gospel album, *One Voice,* in 2005.

The cast of *The Jamie Foxx Show* included Garrett Morris (far left).

20

the R-rated comedy *Booty Call* (1997).
Recently, he was asked why he took the role.
"Man, tryin' to stay in the game," he said.
"Just tryin' to stay in the game."

The movie isn't Oscar material. It doesn't
pretend to be great art. But this raunchy film
is one of the funniest movies of the 1990s.

Steamin'

Jamie knew that if he was going to be an
A-list actor, he needed to work with A-list
directors. He got his chance when Oliver
Stone gave him a leading role in the 1999
movie *Any Given Sunday*. This drama about
pro football was a great opportunity for
Jamie. But he almost didn't get the role.

Jamie likes to tell the story of the first
time he met Stone. The director was not
impressed. After Foxx finished his tryout,
Stone said "OK, well, acting is definitely
not what you do." Jamie felt lucky when
he heard Stone had given him a bit
part in the film.

Their next meeting couldn't
have been more different.
Stone was having trouble

Fact File

Jamie did more than act in
Any Given Sunday. He helped
write the movie's title song, and
he produced it and performed on
it, too. He also put together the
music video "My Name Is Willie."

casting the part of quarterback "Steamin'" Willie Beamen. He needed an actor who could look convincing calling the plays and throwing the football.

"I need somebody that knows how to play quarterback," Stone said. Jamie had been a star quarterback in high school, and he had a ready answer. "Mr. Stone," he said, "I can honestly tell you. There's nobody on this set that knows more about football than I do."

Foxx on Football

In 2000, Jamie talked about pro football and *Any Given Sunday* with *Sport* magazine. "Well, you know what you get when it's an Oliver Stone film. There's a lot of looking at what football's really like. A lot of times people look at the NFL and think it's very posh and polished. But it's a business."

"It can get real dirty and ugly," he added. "But at the same time ... football brings everybody together. Fathers, sons, families, Sundays.... Hopefully, people will be able to see all that. Be able to see the controversy in football, but also see the good things it does."

In this scene from *Any Given Sunday*, QB Willie Beamen gets some advice from his coach, played by Al Pacino.

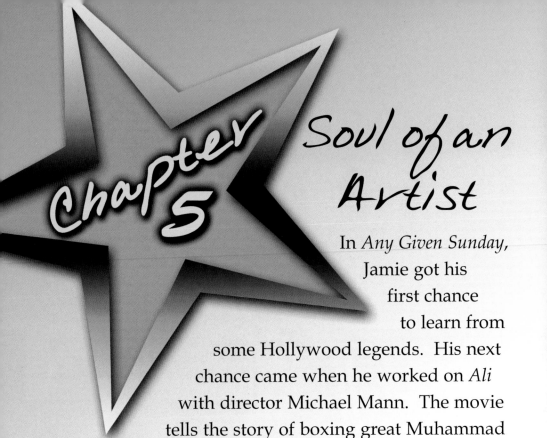

Chapter 5

Soul of an Artist

In *Any Given Sunday*, Jamie got his first chance to learn from some Hollywood legends. His next chance came when he worked on *Ali* with director Michael Mann. The movie tells the story of boxing great Muhammad Ali. Jamie plays Ali's cornerman, Drew "Bundini" Brown.

At first, Mann had his doubts, just as Stone did. The buff Jamie didn't look a bit like the pot-bellied Bundini. But Will Smith, who played Ali, put in a good word, and Jamie delivered.

Mann had no doubts when he made his next film, *Collateral*. For this movie, he cast Jamie as Max. Max is a quiet cabdriver who lives in his own private

Fact File

Michael Mann created the *Miami Vice* TV series in the 1980s. Jamie has signed up with Colin Farrell for a *Miami Vice* movie, written and directed by Mann.

Party Time

Jamie won't deny that he loves to party. He says what he really wants is to do great things with great people — and have fun, too. He told a reporter for *Variety*, "If you are not having fun and the people around you are not having fun, then what's it all worth?"

How about a long-term relationship? In 2004, he talked with *People* magazine about finding a woman he could trust. "Is she being real right now? Or is it because I'm doing the flicks? Or because I'm hot right now? What is it? ... The young lady that I date now ... she doesn't care about that. I know she digs me because she was there when I was just trying to figure out how to get from point A to point B."

One of many tense moments from *Collateral*, in which Jamie stars with Tom Cruise

Jamie's work in *Ray* showed the spirit and soul of Ray Charles.

world. One night, Max picks up Vincent, a hired killer played by Tom Cruise. At first, Max doesn't realize that Vincent is planning a one-night killing spree. When Max finds out what Vincent is doing, he has to find a way to stop him.

The film is full of violence and tension. It is also beautiful to watch. Cruise is at the top of his game. But the real eye-opener is Jamie's performance.

Remembering Ray

Movie fans were impressed with Jamie in *Collateral*. But they were amazed by his work in *Ray*. This movie tells the story of musician Ray Charles. Ray went blind as a child, but he didn't let his blindness stop him. He was a gifted singer, pianist, and songwriter. Ray sang everything — gospel, R&B, country, blues, and jazz. But he had a soulful sound that was all his own.

Ray wasn't a perfect person. The film shows him cheating on his wife. It shows him doing drugs, too. It also shows him overcoming his drug habit later in life.

In the movie, Jamie looked like Ray. He talked like Ray. He walked like Ray. He sang like Ray. But his performance was more than just imitation. He worked hard to show how the blind singer had to depend on his other senses to get around. Jamie's years of piano training helped him capture the way Ray's fingers moved on a keyboard. He created a flesh-and-blood portrait of a troubled genius.

Fact File

Jamie met Ray Charles before filming for *Ray* started. Ray died in June 2004, a few months before the movie came out.

For his work in *Ray*, Jamie won more than an Oscar — he won respect. Taylor Hackford was the director on *Ray*. He says it's important to understand that Jamie is serious about his acting. "When you meet Jamie, he's a cool cat," Hackford told *Variety*. "Whatever his kind of all partying style is, forget it. This is a man who is incredibly smart and who is totally committed."

Backstage at the Academy Awards, on Jamie's big night.

Time Line

1967 Eric Morlon Bishop is born on December 13 in Terrell, Texas.

1990 While performing at comedy clubs in Los Angeles, Eric changes his name to Jamie Foxx.

1991 Joins the cast of the TV show *In Living Color*.

1994 Releases his first music CD, *Peep This*.

1996 *The Jamie Foxx Show* starts its five-year TV run.

1999 Jamie plays quarterback Willie Beamen in *Any Given Sunday*.

2001 Has a featured role as Drew "Bundini" Brown in the film *Ali*.

2004 Stars in the movies *Redemption*, *Collateral*, and *Ray*.

2005 Wins an Oscar for Best Actor for his performance in *Ray*.

Glossary

cornerman — in boxing, the person who helps a boxer between rounds of a fight.

duet — a musical number for two people.

Grammy — an award given by the music industry.

impression — in comedy, an exaggerated imitation of somebody famous.

mimicry — the act of imitating a person, often for comic effect.

NAACP — the initials for the National Association for the Advancement of Colored People. This organization fights for civil rights and equality in the United States. It was founded in 1909.

nominated — named or suggested as a candidate for a particular honor or position.

Oscar — another name for an Academy Award, which is given by the movie industry.

R&B — short for rhythm and blues. R&B includes many kinds of African American pop music.

sitcom — short for situation comedy, a kind of weekly TV comedy series. It usually has the same cast of characters each week.

To Find Out More

Books

Funny Bones: Comedy Games and Activities for Kids.
Lisa Bany-Winters (Chicago Review Press)

Ray: A Tribute to the Movie, the Music, and the Man.
Taylor Hackford and Jamie Foxx (Newmarket Press)

Working in Music and Dance. My Future Career
(series). Margaret McAlpine (Gareth Stevens)

Videos

Journeys in Black: Jamie Foxx
(Black Entertainment Television) NR

The Jamie Foxx Show: The Complete First Season
(Warner) NR

Ray (Universal) PG-13

Redemption (Fox) NR

Web Sites

The Internet Movie Database
www.imdb.com
Facts about movies and the people who make them

Ray Charles
www.raycharles.com
The official web site for Ray Charles

Index

About the Author

Geoffrey M. Horn has been a fan of music, movies, and sports for as long as he can remember. He has written more than a dozen books for young people and adults, along with hundreds of articles on many different subjects. He lives in southwestern Virginia, in the foothills of the Blue Ridge Mountains, with his wife, their collie, and four cats. He dedicates this book to the Horn cousins and to the memory of his Uncle Phil.